ARROW POINTING NORTH

Also by David Dodd Lee

DOWNSIDES OF FISH CULTURE

ARROW POINTING NORTH

DAVID DODD LEE

FOUR WAY BOOKS

NEW YORK

Editorial Office
Four Way Books
PO Box 535, Village Station
New York, NY 10014
www.fourwaybooks.com

Library of Congress
Catalog Card Number: 2001 132486

ISBN 1-884800-41-6

Book Design: Brunel
Cover Art: Wendy Goldberg

This book is manufactured in the United States of America and printed on acid-free paper.

Four Way Books is a division of Friends of Writers, Inc., a Vermont-based not-for-profit organization. We are grateful for the assistance we receive from individual donors and private foundations.

Publication of this book was
supported by a generous grant
from the CIRE Foundation.

ACKNOWLEDGMENTS

Thanks to the editors of the following magazines and anthologies for helping some of the poems in this book, or versions of them, see the light of day:

American Literary Review	Losing Everything
Crab Creek Review	I Want to Be Buried
Heliotrope	The Black Bass
	Finding Mushrooms at Dawn Along the Paw Paw River
Isle Review	Ohio Fever
	The Owl Left a Feather in the Bucket Again
The Ledge	Meteorology
Lilliput Review	A History of Owls
Nerve	After Diagnosis
	Instead
Perihelion	Vanishing Point
Passages North	Starlight
	Inside/Outside
	Detour: Tampa
Prairie Schooner	At the Hospital
	At the Moment of Death
Rattle	Window Drive-In
	An Arrow Pointing North
	Sometimes I'd Sit in a Field
Slope	The Wedge
	The Beauty of the Present Tense
	Burning Leaves
	Summer
Sundog	Night Juniper
Talking River Review	Out at Sea
Washington Square	The Lighthouse
Willow Springs	Talking about Snow All Night
New Poems from the Third Coast	Cigarette Break

Four of these poems appeared in a chapbook, *Wilderness,* published in 2000 by March Street Press. My thanks to Robert Bixby.

I wish to express my gratitude to the Irving S. Gilmore Emerging Artist Foundation, and to the Arts Council of Greater Kalamazoo, who supported me with grants while I wrote this book.

My heartfelt thanks go out to Gretchen Mattox, Jonathan Johnson, Vito Aiuto and Donna Munro for their unending support and encouragement.

for Marilyn, with Love

CONTENTS

WINDOW DRIVE-IN

All night long giant men and women
move their hands over each other
while I sleep. One combs his fingers
through a woman's hair and they both lie down out of sight.
Her white dress flutters.

It blows down a slope
and settles on top of the flat slow river.
A helicopter chops holes in the paper clouds.

All the while, armored fish chase one another
around my bedroom,
down the hall and into the kitchen—
they bang against the hanging pots and pans,
swim in and out of windows.

OHIO FEVER

(Fremont and Marietta)

It wasn't thunder I heard
But a woman in a white T-shirt wading the river
I remember washing her
Belly
Each leg
I gave her my necklace
Making love is like drinking
She said
She slept
Like a tarantula
On the horizon of a dream
She told me my arms
Smelled the same as my sex
She put her hair in a ponytail
I held it
I washed all of her
She smelled like the lake
Her neck in the mirror was long as a gazelle's
She gave me a fish
The fish was a rainbow
Full of mudpuppies
She rested her hands on my shoulders
She touched my neck
Getting me to kneel
She took off her shoes
And reached into a brown sack of feathers
She said think of a swan
A white deer
Of lightbulbs and rain

I smelled perfume
Rising from the warm pillow
It wasn't thunder
A woman had drowned in that river

FINDING MUSHROOMS AT DAWN ALONG THE PAW PAW RIVER

Dawn unearths them,
naked and blind as grubs
inside their frosted vestments. The underwater gravel
flashes, tongues of alabaster,
while the deer move in two-toed spirals away from center.
And the fish, small coffins,

swim upstream in a blur,
like thoughts, like the ghost
of a print after a man has kissed a woman
on the cheek—a whisper of salt
bathing the tip of his tongue—or the suddenly weightless

drift in the bones
of their hands
as they pick—filling their pockets—the honeycombed
bodies of fruit,
leaving the soft white stems like miniature human ears
behind, in the woods.

THE LIGHTHOUSE

I don't come clean easy and I don't
stink much although I've known a few shadows who do.
They live in the brightness. They die there.

I used to think, no. Let the lighthouse spin round and round . . .
Let the voice
leak out of the fog. Sometimes by simply standing

I create more others, shirts in the window,
breakfast of invisible stars. The lake shifts under its altar
of wet sills, like a starling woman, feathers

over her arms moving away through the rain,
small clouds. My brother, almost born,
calls me on most of this stuff. *You're talking to the furnace again,*

he might say. Or *What's with the flashlight pendulum?*
But he loves the lake the way I do, no words,
but also no pins in a map. He lives in the brightness,

which I sometimes glimpse when the lighthouse
(or my watch) glows in the dark.
It's like a light shining through water, a harbor.

THE UNIVERSE AS ELLIPSIS

My good intentions felt ruinously wet.
I spoke & a flag with a skull of embroidery
leapt into the morning.

I woke on a bed,
a promontory,
overlooking a field of sparkling tray tables—
incision supplies, the heads of men and women
stuck on each
beside soft white bowls of warm water.
Then nothing for months.

When a black hole implodes
we're not sure, are we,
what's on the other side, what manifestation
waits like star-burned mobius strips
amid the dimensionless voices intersecting there?

But for now, we're here, all in a row,
waiting for the decapitations
& once in a lifetime rebates to kick in, here,
where a feather
proposes its name is really *flame*,
& where a man with a blade & boxes of betadine pads
turns to look
at the soft skin just under
another quickly contracting pupil.

I hypothesize—
before all is said and done,
after the blaze of several years' shadows

begins to blur like spokes—
that the man will then turn the gleaming scalpel upon himself,
leaving each dormant head
with its recycled thoughts—; how happy am I,
what's next to *want,*
if I were able to look into a mirror would I
even have eyes?

UNRETRIEVABLE LOVE POEM

(Rocky Mount, North Carolina)

1.

Little comes through—burned all up. He squeezed shut his eyes,
leaking like pools, a child's, freshly slit. A bead of blood hangs
from a pure black lash.

2.

The fields outside are studded with garbage cast-off
in the snow-broken tufts of grass. It's sunny, the white hills
marbled with dirt and ice.
Who are you, who can't even cradle the child in your lap
without fear of retribution?

(Let him beat on the boy with a branch,
pinch him with scissors,
he'll never suck her dry.)

A woman stands holding her child, barely visible through the
falling snow,
nowhere to walk but along the river . . .

3.

Hell, the *fish* don't *care,* apoplectic with sleep,
nosed deep into the mud of the bank, eyes snowed with
an absence
of hunger.
Even then, I knew
a stupid conceit when I heard it. Let's tip another beer.

4.

In Holton my girlfriend
walks home after work. It's dark but the trail's a bright ring
around Ergang Lake,
moonlight splashing off water lilies,

overturned white spiders opening their legs,
dying . . .

There's a scar in a curve
where the water ebbs back, cues of reckoning,
white petals like swans
sailing over the crests of a wake.

5.

I dream our child lies in a dark copse surrounded by brown
    birds
with long beaks and blue eyes.

6.

And the phone that was ringing
in the woods is real,
shining like the moon nailed to the trunk of a hollow tree.

SOMETIMES I'D SIT IN THE FIELD

There is a town in the South
where as a boy I played in the Drive-in that was like a desert
of broken down cars and hot weeds,
steel posts wearing headsets the wind cried through.

I'd sit in the field behind the barbed wire fence
and watch X-rated movies,
listen to the car horns, the muffled, indecipherable words
of the actors, whose huge bodies

lit up the sky like searchlights.

THE BLACK BASS

My hand became my father's hand
that day,
for a second or two, as I lifted the fish, and I could feel his loneliness,
my father's, like mine,

a horse in a stall spooked by guttering candles,
the popping and black smoke, the quivering flanks.

And if a horse, in *its* loneliness, couldn't manage
to speak, what difference did it make?
What could he say? Tell a flickering candle *Burn true?*

Then I thought of my mother, standing in a field with flames
in her hair. She was surrounded by deer, statues
in a circle around her.

DRUNKS

Thunder. It's November, dusk, raining.
Soon it will be cold.
The houses look naked (unapologetically

streaming electrical wires),
and the trees drip, their branches empty of walnuts,
which lie in the grass, rotting . . .

I suggest you walk politely
away from my front door
without trying to peer in or call out my name,

the way we used to as children,
from bicycles.
Please don't make me get up out of this chair.

METEOROLOGY

A man wakes on a too-small continent
and suddenly he is afraid of the dark bearing down
on the city. He's afraid that one day
he will turn his head
to find towering walls of water rushing toward
him from both horizons,
oceans swallowing even this particular neighborhood
ostensibly tucked so safely away
in a corner of the Midwest.
He reaches over to touch his wife, who is hot,
who has begun to snore like a small boat idling
she is sleeping so deeply.
He likes how her thighs
seem to hold onto his head when he eats her,
trapping him, refusing to let him go
until *she's* ready. The two motors of their hearts
rev, snap at each other,
hammer away at the inflows of blood.
He hates his job, and she knows this
and when she lets him go
she lets him have her completely.
He thinks of this, and of his many sins
and of the time he has left
to make her truly happy. Television
and radio waves scumble across the dark ceiling
in the bedroom, and he watches them,
born afraid, he suddenly realizes,
of everything. Sometimes, the robins poking
around in the leaves of some instantly too-calm evening,
she takes his hand inside both of hers.
The watery distance shines like a mirror

he sneaks looks at over her shoulder.
At some point he leaves to scribble an idea or two
about the one who loves dirt, the one who eats light;
folds the small piece of paper,
the words like echoes disappearing into themselves,
and slips into his shirt pocket
the small white rectangle of what he presently feels—
the way she reaches
across to touch him on the blue lawn, claiming him,
claiming even that part of him. Sunday and clear sky.
Birds in the long grass, listening.
A truck thunders over one or another
of the long-distance highways and leaves begin
blowing backwards. There's still no sign of rain.

DETOUR: TAMPA

And the dolphin? It still resembles a shark.
My father, who's a swallow (or a sandwich)
looks out a doctor's window and says he feels a weight-
lessness in one ball, a harbinger of things to come.

My mother sings a cappella in the bathtub.
I remember the singing more than I remember
what the two of them looked like, together, even
though I suspect the large windows
helped me to see what was away from there.

A beautiful, beautiful—on a sunny day—piece of turquoise
  ocean.

The Gulf, somebody corrected me once.

IRON MOUNTAIN, DAUGHTER

(a car crash)

Days like the blip of a flashcube
and night

Night
left to dry on a dock

Dock—field *of bright yellow flowers*

Go forth   Multiply

Wake up underground . . .

*

Perhaps the years run deeper
than we care to remember . . .

Some lisp like history

Some smell like sad fish

I awoke in a river of dream-softened flowers so

HAPPY . . .

"She can talk
but she will never be able to hear you again"

UNRETRIEVABLE LOVE POEM (#2)

1.

A girl I saw at the local supermarket
had thick black eyelashes full of blood.

he couldn't get the pee to come out
cool dusk
a deer with its head above water
dust on the Crucifix

She was confined to a wheelchair.

2.

After slow slow sex my lover falls asleep,
the sawing of her breath
like scissors cutting construction paper.

3.

Sometimes the snow drifts over and past the garbage, blanketing the rills
that lead back to an abandoned apple orchard.

A creek flows freely through the grove all winter.

If you go back far enough you can find hard apples
covered with snow, pink and imperfect, still bunched in the branches.

4.

I remember the bicycle wheel spinning
and spinning, clotted with leaves,
and the harbor of the neighbors' lawns blowing with flames.
A tarantula pissed all over my hand.

A second doctor
pulled a brown recluse, the tarantula's son,
out of my crippled sister's ear.

LOSING EVERYTHING

This time of year
the yard is dark, and long. No use sitting
in the house, all the lights on,
watching crows fill the dead elm,
everyone knows you're unhappy—
a little *cracked,* a single dirge spinning round and round
on the same ineluctable turntable
(a little sand thrown into the works)
you first played T. Rex on,
the black frying pan
you stole from a trunk at your grandfather's
the weekend of his stroke
your only mirror. As the music plays
you stare at the pan dangling over
the sink facing the front lawn
that is like a record turning, like a house bursting
into flames again and again,
like a window with black wings
swallowing the rooms you've long outgrown.
It's snowing outside again,
the flock of crows you reach out to touch
now only a few feet away,
each with a bare lightbulb reflected
in one obsidian eye, each with an oily shine
of metal in wet feathers, each with no voice,
no pulse, cold as painted bronze,
cold as the lawn
you can no longer see through the smoke.

WILDERNESS

He never looked back, even after the lights blinked out,
one by one in a cold rain . . .

He raised off one knee, stood in the mist
and tried reading the woods. The view from an airplane
    revealed that he
was at the center of something, a place where four trails

converged in a scrubby pine field, and the man on the ground
sensed this, took off his hat, looked up at the sky.

Dusk falling, a huge moth
covering the eyes of the certified dead, who lay
in a Cadillac mortuary. Water dripping,
rows of syringes, scalpels gleaming

The man walked around his truck, making
a path out of briars and grass, a widening circle. He was looking
for something to pick up, bring home.

A mortician inserted his needle,
pressed the plunger
and the corpse exhaled

After a while the man stopped in the middle of a dusty field,
wiped his brow
with his sleeve. The last person he talked to said only that she'd

met a man on a deer run wearing a Red Sox cap.
He said he was having trouble remembering the way.
Could she kindly point him in the direction of the river?

BURNING LEAVES

(Brandywine Lake)

And I think, after I open my eyes to the morning's pale
Dissolve, I understand the labyrinthine
Blood laughing
At the room standing upside down
One millisecond
Before consciousness blots out the indescribable beyond

Then the countless leaves. A windbreaker (white with a blue
lining)
A melody, the words of which have disappeared

You know, don't you
You even thought to say so once, and turned it around in your mind
Then kept it

THE WEDGE

In a wide, white room, I've been refusing to cooperate
It's true

But yesterday, Monday, I spent the morning logging in deer-kill data
At the fish hatchery

A single orange leaf floats over the ice-blue pond . . .

A little fur the color of rust
Coming away bright on my fingers—the animals' lips pried
Making them look as if they may begin screaming

SUMMER

Even now, I see them.
The way their hair drifts toward the top of the water, eyes half-open.
Shining like paint, like the wedge of an apple.

Like a gestural splash of light,
A chinook salmon
Emerging not ten feet from the boat.

Someday, an urgent spring will poke its lime-green shoots
Through the cemetery of those boys' ribs . . .

Spiders turn to dust inside their webs. A woman
Begins to move beneath me,
Groaning,
Like a swingset made of wood.

AT THE MOMENT OF DEATH

Woke after a nightmare. Saw
Waves, light pouring into my room.

Knew all was temporary. Slow fade
On the roar of the sea—Oh well:

Time for the rudderless snail
To coast over my grave in his shining body.

The polyphemus (or is it an owl suddenly)
Opens its wings in the moonlight.

READING THE BIBLE AT WORK

I've got the sweats
full of fear. I've got love and an appetite,
war on the page.

Missiles fly across the desert.
A computer that has worried pisses out a tiny electric dot.
But then a guy with a wisp of a mustache comes to the window

to get six trachea tubes.
I don't know what will save us.
I cling to my hunger; I open the book.

HUMMINGBIRD, NUMBER 17

This is not the first time I've sat down here,
far from it. The altar of birth, and its song birds,
its chorus of beautiful animals. I
was born. Things slowly came into focus—
an occasional upside-down image
of a man building the stone fence of his later days falling
into place
piece by piece. But for years the frame

actually narrowed. I saw leaves and trees, gray leaves and rain,
white snow, white sun. I'm still most comfortable watching
birds, so other are they, like a wind full of punctuation marks

conjugating the trees, cutting the world into quarters,
and eighths,
small paragraphs. A single desultory ant
meanders over the wooden desert
of a picnic table
and stops to check out the environs
from the dome of a bolt. No doubt
my sister fussed with her sandwich, stuck it inside
her glass of milk, stared at my mother,
her face not yet of one piece,
her lips like a red red crayon . . .

I remember every hummingbird I've ever seen, for example.

A HISTORY OF OWLS

Late afternoons, in the fall, while the children
Chase each other with their paper horses,
The rest of the town dreams through another long nap

The Douglas firs tower over
Slow moving glaciers
Flowing down out of another time

While the bones of digested songbirds
Thud down
Onto soft green beds, pine needles and moss

QUARTER NOTES

What are we to do with you, Birdsong,
when our heads are so goddamned packed
we see musical notations
cluttering like ribbons of eels that wind through the trees?
And Moon, chalice of gold, what to do
with your liquid like blood that splatters
round in the dark
in the faces of walkers, surprising them.
Except that it's water, just a late-night sprinkler.
Sprinkler, or moonlight—once you fess up
it's beside the point. That first weighty orb
blows its heft over the path of your crow's feet.
A dog barks. He's startled, too.
And everyone's waking
to the tinkle of quarter notes bouncing off awnings,
whole notes like hail.
There's too much coming in,
and the dead don't like it one bit, that we're forgetting,
that we know we're forgetting
when in moments
we lose our place in a tone or a shadow
of chill & turn
to see, as if made radiant by sudden green
bolts of lightning,
the bones of our ancestors twirling like Calders from the torched
branches of elms, which we've also forgotten,
razed, burned to the ground on a wet day in 1969,
Jefferson Airplane filling the airwaves,
the smoke of certain careless summers
past, & you wish you could set fire to a joint, the sweet
smell of not giving a shit,

but will settle for today's burning leaves,
a formerly all-day job lazily threaded with long meandering pauses
spent leaning on the blunt end of a rake,
a too-long conversation with a neighbor perhaps,
instead of this blurring on through—as if beached—
the old & prematurely historical
catalogues of our presently long-ago loves.

STARLIGHT

All day long smoke drifted through the lilacs
and the idea of that was so beautiful
I wasn't surprised when some of my neighbors
came out of their houses and wandered
through the woods, looking for something.
That night over Brandywine Lake
the full moon froze the silhouettes
of geese flying north and the smell
of burned flowers wafted through the screens.
It was as if one might live forever, seeing these things,
feeling them flow, one into another,
like the river of bees that streamed all summer long
out a knothole in the side of the house,
comets blown through a black hole, or like miniature
aircraft, dispersed among the trunks of trees
eventually to be lost in the darkness of nightfall.

INSIDE/OUTSIDE

You see the lake now, as every morning,
driving to work, the way it just lies there, under ice,
under the zagging shadows of trees without leaves,
some of the boathouse doors

askew from a winter's battering, but somebody's
boathouse, white, for instance, brown trim like a little
home. Like your home, your love,

your circular dreams, your present idea-of-self,
your lake-full-of-fish self, a body of water only a mile from end to end
and round as a full moon,
the big paper circle propped in the street you accidentally drive

your car through,
everyone cheering, but the paper is ice and the ice
becomes a blizzard

with a hole in its corner,
and your family, they love you, only their love is in slow-
motion and no one's aware of the thick carp glancing off your
   windshield.
Every morning you walk out the door

with your lunch in a sack.
It's nothing like a painting, although sometimes your wife
draws the face of a laughing rabbit on the brown paper

while you're upstairs dressing.
Door, lake, boathouse, stoplight, first cigarette.
Long streams of snow blowing off your roof like a wake.
Big paper bag with a drawing of a rabbit on it

you hit going fifty.

I WANT TO BE BURIED

When it's time, I want to be buried under a river,
so that eventually my bones become
a place for fish to hide, small ones, like the dull
fathead minnow or maybe a creek chub, plain
as a white piece of paper.
I would like to be structure, instead of a headstone.
It might take a hundred—maybe a thousand—years
but I want to be buried deep under the current
of some hurtling stream of water
so eventually a crayfish, if he feels like it, can climb up a rib
once in a while, oversized claw in tow,
to just look around or wave good-bye to his friend.
Sticklebacks, water boatmen, mud puppies
could all find refuge in my eye sockets
in the event someone larger—say, a steelhead—goes hunting.
I would like to be structure
for pike, visiting from warm water estuaries,
my hip like a bottle opener for prying
out treble hooks. All winter long I'd be surrounded
by pines heavy with snow, a few ice-capped logs sporting
what look like helmets,
an occasional crow crossing overhead,
a piece of somebody's lost shadow.

AT THE HOSPITAL

Those unbelievable new faces!
Who knows what they see,
What they think when
The world fans out before them

And they have to lie there,
Wriggling, stung by this new light,
Drifting away from the old. They're nothing like the dead
Who on occasion I've looked in on

(I've got a key) in the morgue and who mostly seem
Far away, memory no longer even a part of the room.
We write what we know
On a chart. Someone looks at a watch.

Look at him. Not even a spark in his head.
While upstairs a baby is beginning to breech.
And this guy—he just keeps getting heavier & heavier
And heavier & heavier . . .

Still, if you ride the elevator a few times
You might begin to notice a resemblance between the man
In the drawer in the basement
And the six-pound girl who's been yanked out amongst us.

She howls with uncertainty. The man burns
With consciouslessness, like a chair, or the clock hanging on the wall
Someone looks at.
Writes down the time of birth.

THE OWL LEFT A FEATHER IN THE BUCKET AGAIN

Love, I saw you once, your handlebars curved against the wind.
I have been sealing many envelopes,
sleeping in corduroy, drinking half & half with a little coffee.
A lantern's been spotted flying over the lake.
In twenty-two cities the comic strips
leak into the daily news—it's all a big joke!
Somehow a candle burns in the vacated grocery store.

A girl with a vaccination scar
entered the local bank wanting a loan for a cemetery plot.
Nobody knew her.
Love, I saw a priest wandering the aisles of K-mart wearing a pea coat.
He had dreadlocks. He was buying CDs.
Mr. Love, please, I bought pillows for the orphanage,

a new bedspread to cover my wife's menstrual stains.
I watched a man give another man the finger in broad daylight.

I'm not alone in this.
The black widows crawl over the tops of mailboxes; ambulances
idle at the end of our road. A red and yellow can
of gasoline appeared in the middle of the football field
last week. It wasn't an accident. Mr. Love, Dear Love,
the bridge is not safe anymore. The swallows are about to revolt.

Quite often they can be seen with something orange in their beaks.
I fear the worst.
An owl left a feather in the bucket again.

CIGARETTE BREAK

It's not the weather, or the fact that two ambulances
have already unloaded their cargo and sit in the emergency drive,
idling. It's sunny, in fact, out here, next to this brick
wall where I'm taking time out for a cigarette
and a cup of coffee, freezing my ass off actually, but happy,
for a few seconds at least, to be out of the basement.
It's not very much, one cigarette, and it's not very heartening
watching sick people struggle through the snow
to smoke one either. Wrapped in an oversized coat,
a woman, whose spindly legs are bare where they meet
her inadequately slippered feet, limps by trailing an IV
that dangles from a portable stand. Whatever I've got waiting
downstairs—the anesthesia cart to inventory, some cardboard boxes
to bale—takes half an hour. I hate that I sometimes hate what I do,
but not because of this sick woman, who,
after feeling her pockets, jabs her chin at me to ask for a light.
She's ugly, and old, a hank of greasy hair
and a mouthful of broken-up teeth. And she won't talk,
doesn't want to I guess. She sucks the flame into her cigarette,
takes a long initial drag, then blows out the smoke.
She stands there hunched over, smoking, and clutching the IV stand
for support. I've been at this job a long time, so this woman's
nothing. One woman expired, right here, last fall, fell over in the middle
of a sentence. They rushed her into the ER on one of those brand
new rolling stretchers, but I heard later she had died almost instantly
from a burst aorta. No big surprise when you work at a hospital.
The sick come in. The sick go out. Sometimes they don't go out.
In the meantime all the healthy people stand around
glimpsing the future, their eyes lit up like a deer's in traffic.
Occasionally a visitor will wail for their loss, like someone
burning in an empty room, a howl you can hear

coming through the vents in the storeroom.
I know I should quit these goddamned cigarettes. But they buy me some time,
somehow, a momentary stay of execution. Then it's
back to the business of filling up bins. I flick my smoke into a snowdrift.
And the woman, who's suddenly listing a little, begins hacking,
doing her best to split her thick winter coat. When she finally
recovers she turns to look at me watching her.
Her eyes are red, wet looking.
It happens again and again, the dead look out of their graves
at the living, not a word needing to be uttered.

OUT AT SEA

And then you find yourself falling through the towering bodies,
Wet with dream-paint,
Little fear of soul
Breezing by in the middle of the night,
That landscape of spectral forms
You glide through, silently, unable
To speak . . .
The passing white blurs of mountain goats,
The graph-like striations in rock . . .

Maybe they'll get your heart beating again,
Like a clock, like a mother's heart,
And like her mother's heart before you were born.
Up you'll come, breaking through walls and walls
Of feathers and glass, re-emerged finally,
Scratched and hairless,
The electrocardiogram
Bobbing once again
Like a tern floating on rough seas.

THE BEAUTY OF THE PRESENT TENSE

(Whitefish Bay Cemetery)

"The dead would like a word with you

They've been waiting for years
cubicle of green grass
Surrounded by a white picket fence

Richard R. Sutton would like to talk to you:

It's nice
What you've done with the place,
Plastic flowers, the headstones lined
In symmetrical rows . . .

And the espalier!

I wish you could hear the mockingbirds the way I do,

The music they make when they gather,
Long watery strains like a chorus of cellos.

Or how a single bird might separate from the flock
And form a bridge that sounds like a dulcimer
Weeping in the middle of the night."

*

The nearby stink of cows in the air
A long time reading between sun and cold willows
Buckets and buckets of bright milk

INSTEAD

Water's leaking into the basement
through mortar, dark in the dark,
like tears,
like the house is in pain.

*

She sleeps most of the time, or else
she's trembling with palsy—but to me
she's grown more beautiful. How can it be other . . .

Her blue eyes shine—

How can she be dying, who fills the bottle
at will, who
when we make love grows warmer and warmer
in my hands?

THE TIME I LOST MY KEYS

The lantern paints the bales
with rain. *Excuse me,* I say to a long long shadow.
Mist. Cold.
At some point I'd been driving a car, I think . . .

Some warm blanket of dream
inside memory this is.

BEFORE

(Tampa, Florida)

Because he could not face what came next,
Mist driven home,
The grass becoming visible, no longer only a word . . .

She stops and looks at the lakes—
How they are white and blue all at once

*

"Look at us, in the mirror," she said. "Who doesn't belong?"

*

The air makes a parabolic shape
Around his mind. Suddenly he's breathing
And it is a *now* breath, the light

Moving closer, *arousing* the lawn. Boats and paintbrushes,
Horseshoe crabs. Sandalwood. A turquoise breeze.

*

She blows him a kiss from the train heading north

TALKING ABOUT SNOW ALL NIGHT

1.

He kissed them, before rubbing snow on the arms
Of the girls
Who'd come back crying
From the lake where they'd been lost on the ice.
Nobody froze or drowned.
Flakes like dust rolled by in a wave,
Blinding them,
And the snow refused to lie down.
That's how they almost froze,

With skates on their feet.
When he eased their cold fingers out of their gloves
He thought of birds being born.

2.

But it's almost summer now.
The piles of snow shrink back over the dirt
And grass.
                    Soon people are leaving cordless phones
On porch railings.
A woman does so so she can walk across the street
And sleep beneath
A row of blossoming dogwoods.
And the voice on the other end of the line
Grows smaller and smaller
Until there is nothing left but a fly
Bumping in lazy circles
Against the dusty garage door's windows.

3.

I once had a dream in which everyone parked
Their cars
In a lot the size of Ohio & left them to rust.
They sat steaming in the fields for months,
The batteries slowly losing their charges, cooling,
One by one the dashboards fading,
Until one night late in October—
He thought he could hear the abandoned cars
Begin whispering to one another . . .

And it sounded like a light rain falling
Or like the soughing of waves
Through an open window
While you're trying to sleep
In a bed
With a woman who's been talking about snow all night,

How beautiful it is in the moonlight
After the city shuts down,
How it causes the deer to poke their noses through the hedges
After wandering like children
Into the suburbs,
Looking for something they're not sure they want to find.

AN ARROW POINTING NORTH

While the man unbuttons her blouse
he watches the clouds
sail through her eyes. She smells his warm breath
that is like a sea blown inland. He dreams he is in bed
with a glass sphere full of snow and a migrating V of plastic geese
only he can hear honking. He looks out the window at a duplicate
   formation,
an arrow pointing north. It is late spring,
the woman beside him sleeping in a full-length wedding gown.
Now he remembers
                                        the noisy parade of cars
trailing streamers and cans, the huge hook-lipped fish.

AFTER DIAGNOSIS

Sometimes I lick her skin and it tastes like hot sand.
She moans, pooling deep into the mattress,
into water—sweat, cum, solidified hair of her nails—
like a breeze coming onshore,
like the leaves springing to life over the lawn.

The shadow of a kingfisher hovers over a still pond.
It grows larger and cooler.
It moves like a hand covering my wife's eyes, bones of pure feeling,
the blind tongue entering the warm cunt.

The roots cracking the house foundation begin to bleed.
The wind scatters vowels like an animal's dream.

NIGHT JUNIPER

Somebody who lives in the house looks out a window.
Carp blink deep in their homemade ponds. And the insects
have all climbed the trunks of various trees to flatten out, disappear.

Over one pond a few bats dive-bomb the freshly emerging mosquitoes,

while water striders continue to scull toward a memory,
the last-remembered sunset . . .

*

So what happens next?
A few voices, somebody's mother laughing over the ethereal dim of a
swimming pool
(earlier there'd been splashing),
a girl at the bus stop whispering to her boyfriend.

VANISHING POINT

Beautiful scallops of painted metal drip in the rain.
Love just keeps smacking
Into these tormented cold mirrors, like leaves
Throwing down their wet brown faces.

Perhaps the moment is inside the woman,
Or contained inside her yet-to-be daughter.
Perhaps I'll find
In a field lassoed by the curves of a stuffed river
The fingerprints of my only love.

Or perhaps I'll simply stand on the horizon
Of a lamplit doorway
And fix my lapel for the duration.
Watch the past fly over the harbor, a missile,
That explodes like an exhalation of paint.

Someone has thoughtfully lined the cold floor
With tissues.
I could live with this kind of never-ending . . .
A vanishing point. A hallway.

David Dodd Lee is the author of *Downsides of Fish Culture* (New Issues Press, 1997), a full-length collection, and *Wilderness* (March Street Press, 2000), a chapbook. His poems have been published in *CutBank, Many Mountains Moving, The Quarterly, Green Mountains Review, Puerto del Sol, Nerve, Hawaii Review, RHINO, Cream City Review, Cimarron Review, Sycamore Review, Willow Springs, Quarterly West, Prairie Schooner, American Literary Review,* and elsewhere. He has been poetry editor at *Passages North* and *Third Coast,* the literary magazine published at Western Michigan University, where he received an MFA in Creative Writing in 1993, and a BFA in Painting in 1986. Together with Donna Munro, he is editor of Half Moon Bay poetry chapbooks. He is currently working as a freelance editor and journalist, and has also worked as a park ranger, fisheries technician, handmade papermaker, and teacher of creative writing, as well as in redistribution in a hospital. He has just completed a novel entitled *Flood.* He lives in Kalamazoo with his wife, Marilyn, and their dog and cat.

The Stahlecker Series

was established in memory of poet Beth Stahlecker, whose book, *Three Flights Up,* was published posthumously by Four Way Books in 1996 (with an afterword by Ellen Bryant Voigt). The series publishes emerging poets, favoring the shorter collection.

More Things in Heaven and Earth
Kurt Brown

Return of the Prodigals
Kurt Brown

Precipice
John Donoghue

Winter Light
Gary Duehr

Whole Sky
Pamela Kircher

Arrow Pointing North
David Dodd Lee

The Harness
Pat Mangan

The Near Surround
Nancy Mitchell

Rogue Apostle
Mary Jane Nealon

Lush
Frazier Russell

Traditions of Bread and Violence
Catherine Sasanov